Color the World
with Kindness

50 Ways to *Brighten* Someone's Day

Tae Lynne

BALBOA
PRESS
A DIVISION OF HAY HOUSE

Balboa Press books may be ordered through booksellers or by contacting:

Balboa Press
A Division of Hay House
1663 Liberty Drive
Bloomington, IN 47403
www.balboapress.com
1 (877) 407-4847

Because of the dynamic nature of the Internet, any web addresses or links contained in this book may have changed since publication and may no longer be valid. The views expressed in this work are solely those of the author and do not necessarily reflect the views of the publisher, and the publisher hereby disclaims any responsibility for them.

The author of this book does not dispense medical advice or prescribe the use of any technique as a form of treatment for physical, emotional, or medical problems without the advice of a physician, either directly or indirectly. The intent of the author is only to offer information of a general nature to help you in your quest for emotional and spiritual well-being. In the event you use any of the information in this book for yourself, which is your constitutional right, the author and the publisher assume no responsibility for your actions.

Cover Design & Illustrations: All original artwork created by Elaine Cooper

All royalties earned from the sale of this book go directly to the Solve ME/CFS Initiative, whose mission is to make ME/CFS understood, diagnosable and treatable.

The Solve ME/CFS Initiative (SMCI)- was founded in 1987 and has established itself as the leading charitable organization dedicated to myalgic encephalomyelitis (ME)/Chronic Fatigue Syndrome (CFS) – also known as chronic fatigue and immune dysfunction syndrome (CFIDS). Learn more at SolveCFS.org

Print information available on the last page.

ISBN: 978-1-5043-6319-8 (sc)
ISBN: 978-1-5043-6320-4 (e)

Balboa Press rev. date: 11/17/2016

Praise

for *Color the World with Kindness*

"Kindness matters. It has always mattered. In today's world, it matters more than ever. Just like the snowball effect, each act of kindness travels into our world, builds upon itself, and ultimately has the potential to create an enormous impact. Tae Lynne suffered a severe and unexpected course change in life. Instead of allowing it to derail her and send her spiraling permanently down the slope of self-pity and despair, she allowed the abrupt change in direction to lead her to something wonderful: a change in purpose. She managed her snowball's force and direction and in doing so, Tae began to change the world, one act of kindness at a time. It's something we *all* can do. Through her warm hearted and soulfully wise book, *Color the World with Kindness*, Tae guides us to use simple, daily acts of kindness to shift our circumstances. If you walk through these pages and practice Tae's suggestions, you will sense a change in your life. Just like the ever increasing snowball, no small act of kindness is ever small. It contributes to growth, change, and magnificence of the whole. *Color the World with Kindness* will help you realize that in extending kindness to others, the brilliance of your own life sparkles and shines."

~Jen Flick, New York Times Best-selling Author: *Eat Pray Love Made Me Do It*, Multiple #1 Amazon Best-selling Author: *Wisdom of Women of Midlife Women 2, Unleash Your Inner Magnificence, 365 Moments of Grace*, and Amazon Best-selling Author, *Cultivating Joy*. More info and events listed @ jenflick.com

"Tae Lynne's book, *Color the Word with Kindness* demonstrates that it does not cost much to show others that you care, although it can mean the world to those that you do. Simply by becoming more aware of the people in your usual day to day activities, you can choose to act kind and make it a more positive world. I recommend reading this book more than once as it has great reminders of how easy spreading kindness can be!"

~Lisa Hutchison LMHC, Author of "Focusing on What We Have" in *Chicken Soup for the Souls The Power of Positive* and *Chicken Soup for the Souls For Mom with Love*, "I Trust in You" in *365 Ways to Connect With Your Soul* and "My True Home" in *Unleash Your Inner Magnificence.*; *Licensed Psychotherapist and Certified Angel Card Reader for Empathic Helpers & Artists.* http://www.lisahutchison.net

"How many times in your life has someone cut you off in traffic, let a door go in your face or jumped ahead of you at the checkout? Even those of us who are well-intentioned end up doing these kinds of things as we rush around frenzied and distracted. Tae Lynne's book reminds us that our 'busyness' isn't all there is to life and if we each take a moment to slow down and share a simple kindness we make the world a better place – and take a mindful moment for ourselves as we do it. Her book is a reminder that it's the little things in life that matter most, and that simple things can have a big impact – often bigger than we know. I wholeheartedly encourage you to be kind to yourself and read *Color the World with Kindness*. It's a breath of fresh air and you won't be disappointed!"

~Kat Tozier, Author of "Finding My Voice" in *Unleash Your Inner Magnificence*; LifeWork Coach at kathleentozier.com; and Founder of the Indomitable Women Academy

"Tae Lynne provides us with 50 actionable ways to brighten someone's day. Kindness is, has been, and will always be our best paintbrush with which to color the world. Nothing changes our day faster than this freely given gift of the heart. Sharing a smile or a kindness is simple, free and non-toxic, benefiting both the sender and receiver. The author's personal stories of kindness are inspiring and highly recommended. A true gem! Let's all join Tae in becoming Kindness Junkies!"

~Debra Oakland, Best-selling Author of *Change your Movie, Change your Life: 7 Reel Concepts for Courageous Change* www.DebraOakland.com

"Color the World with Kindness is a force for good that calls our attention to what truly matters in a world that is more focused on fear and separation than on fellowship and love. Tae Lynne shares beautiful stories and ideas for filling our lives with kindness, compassion, and generosity and reminds us that it takes so little to make a real difference. I saw myself in many of these stories and after reading this book, I am inspired to reach to do even more. Every one of us can be a light to brighten someone's life in some way every single day. How beautiful it is that in giving of ourselves, our own lives are synchronously enriched with peace, harmony, and happiness. With every kindness, we honor the essence of who we really are and open up to boundless possibility."

~Shelley Lundquist, Self-Mastery & Success Coach at www. shelleylundquist.com and co-author of best-selling books including the *Inspiration for a Woman's Soul collection: Choosing Happiness, Cultivating Joy, Gratitude & Grace,* as well as *Unleash Your Inner Magnificence, 365 Ways To Connect With Your Soul,* and *365 Moments of Grace.*

"There is great power in random acts of kindness as Tae Lynne so beautifully demonstrates in her book *Color the World with Kindness: 50 Ways to Brighten Someone's Day.* Not only does she provide wonderful (and easy) examples for how to show kindness to others, she also incorporates inspirational quotes along the way. A warm and delightful read!"

~Sheila Callaham is a best-selling, cross-genre author who also blogs about self-empowerment, spirituality, and humor every week at SheilaCallaham.com.

"*Color the World with Kindness* by Tae Lynne is a book you'll want to buy for your friends and keep a copy on your nightstand. Reading through each quote and each act of kindness is like receiving a bouquet of wild flowers for no particular reason. Tae reminds us how easy and effortless it is to be kind with no strings attached."

~Peggy Nolan, Author of "Can't Die Mom," the award winning flash fiction story, "The Hunger," and the co-author of four Amazon best-selling books, *Inspiration for a Woman's Soul: Choosing Happiness, Inspiration for a Woman's Soul: Cultivating Joy, The Wisdom of Midlife Women,* and *365 Ways to Connect With Your Soul.* www.peggynolan.com

"Life has a way of providing us with unexpected circumstances. Tae Lynne shares her personal story of experiencing a combination of debilitating illnesses and how her courage to heal transformed into becoming the Kindness Junkie. *Color the World with Kindness: 50 Ways to Brighten Someone's Day* is a great book for exploring the various ways to integrate kindness to self, and others, into your life."

~C.K. Kochis, Publisher of Elements for a Healthier Life Magazine www. elementsforahealthierlife.com

"My advance copy of Tae Lynne's new book arrived on the heels of a national tragedy. Savor her anecdotes: they're a reminder that by increasing awareness and developing some other simple habits, everyone can help make the world a bit more user-friendly. Making a difference doesn't always need to be difficult."

~Andrea Patten, Author of *The Inner Critic Advantage: Making Peace With the Noise in Your Head* and *What Kids Need to Succeed: Four Foundations of Adult Achievement.* http://AndreaPatten.com

"I LOVE this book. It is a perfect tool for anyone who is looking for ways to spread kindness and are not sure how. This book is a real page-turner; I could not put it down. Our world needs a lot more "Kindness Junkies." I hope this book will encourage and empower others the way it did for me. Such inspiration!"

~Karen Palmer, Best-selling Author of *GlobalKindness Going Viral* and *The Secret to Puppy Love*

Dedication

This book is dedicated to the multitude of people who have blessed my life over the years.

Most importantly, to my late mother who reminded me to always be kind. I thank her for serving as a living example of kindness throughout my life.

To my family for always being there for me, even when you don't necessarily understand me!

To my friends, some of who I have known for weeks, months, or years. Others of you who have crossed my path for mere moments. You have all left a profound impact on my outlook, my soul, and my sense of purpose.

A special thank you to all the inspiring authors and coaches within my supportive tribe. Your advice, support, and assistance has been invaluable.

And finally, to my loving partner, F.P., for his encouragement, patience, and support. Thank you for understanding my desire to create something from the heart - no matter how many years it took to get to completion.

Introduction

This little book is meant to be an inspirational guide for anyone struggling to renew their self-worth, improve their self-esteem, and discover their purpose in life.

I hope that in reading it, you understand that everyone can find meaning and joy in their lives by giving to others. *There is no better feeling than giving when nothing is expected in return.* Remember, kindness is not hard or time-consuming....it only takes 60 seconds!

When my career was derailed by a chronic illness seven years ago, I struggled with depression, despair, and self-pity. I had been a vivacious, active, "Type A," driven woman who followed the American dream of climbing the corporate ladder. Unable to have children, my career was my focus. When I could no longer work, I suddenly felt like a failure because I could no longer make a meaningful contribution to society in the way I had always wanted.

During times of struggle, it's natural to think "Why me?" or "What is the point of living like this?" or "What do I have to offer the world?" I get it. I understand the pain and feelings of low self-esteem and lack of value.

However, when I began to reflect on the good feelings I had experienced while volunteering when I was healthy, my thoughts began to shift. I enjoyed helping the elderly, the disabled, and many pet rescue organizations. Despite my pain and low energy levels, I began to volunteer with a local hospice organization. Although it was often difficult to maintain the one to two hour weekly commitment, the time spent giving to someone in a less fortunate position made me grateful for what I *still* possessed.

My mind-set shifted further as I began practicing acts of kindness to everyone I came into contact with...a customer service agent on the telephone, a grocery store clerk, a stranger on the street.

I realized that no matter what we are experiencing in our own lives, we are put on this planet for a purpose. Perhaps my purpose was not to raise the bottom line of a corporation's profits, but to raise the consciousness of others to spread kindness in the world.

Use this book as a tool to see what you can do differently in your day-to-day activities. After each act of kindness, there is a reflection question for you to ponder and make a kindness plan you can easily implement.

Don't forget to start with a little self-kindness. If you are struggling with a physical or emotional issue, don't be too hard on yourself. If you aren't kind to yourself first, you'll never know how to be kind to others.

I'd love to connect with you. Please follow my journey at 60SecondstoKindness.com and join my Kindness Junkie community by signing up for the free monthly newsletter.

"Kindness is free.....don't be frugal with it."

~ Tae Lynne

1

Offer to walk your elderly neighbor's dog.

I live in a complex with many senior citizens, all of whom seem to have dogs. One particular woman had a bad hip and walked with a cane. She still managed to walk her little white poodle every day, albeit very slowly.

One morning after walking my dog in an unexpected snow storm, I noticed slippery ice patches under the three inches of snow. I knew this could be treacherous for my neighbor. Seeing that her window blinds were not yet pulled up for the day, I knocked on her door and offered to walk her dog, Molly. Still in her nightgown and her hair a mess, her eyes filled with tears as she graciously thanked me.

I knew my instinct to help had been correct. I left feeling warm in spite of the cold.

How could you be of assistance to an elderly neighbor this week?

_____

_____

_____

_____

_____

"It is the characteristic of the magnanimous man to ask no favor but to be ready to do kindness to others."

~ Aristotle

2

**Buy a dozen roses on Valentine's Day and give them out
unexpectedly to the special women in your life – friends, sisters,
aunts, and neighbors. Enjoy the radiant smile you receive in return.**

One year, a female friend hosted a "Single Gal's Valentine's Day Dinner" for eight women at her home. She invited various women whom she had met during the previous six months. Everyone brought something to add to the meal and we ended up with quite a sumptuous feast.

Our spread included several kinds of cheese and crackers, fruit, shrimp cocktail, curried chicken, grilled pork chops, fried rice, salad, sautéed spinach in garlic, strawberries stuffed with whipped cream and chocolate, cheesecake - and wine - lots of wine!

One of the ladies brought a gorgeous bouquet of roses and handed them out to each woman, even though she only knew the hostess. This touching surprise, on what can be a single gal's most *dreaded* day of the year, brought love and light to the occasion. Smiles, kisses, and hugs were shared by the entire group. Everyone declared it the best Valentine's Day they had ever had.

*Do you have special women in your life who have supported and uplifted you
in times of need? List a few ways you could reach out to show your appreciation
and support in return.*

_____

_____

_____

_____

_____

"One can pay back the loan of gold, but one dies forever in debt to those who are kind."

~ Malayan Proverb

3

**If you own a snow blower, clear your neighbor's
driveway without being asked.**

My father is 87 and lives alone. As often as my siblings and I visit,
we cannot be there for him all of the time. He is lucky enough to have a
neighbor living directly across the street who keeps an eye on him. Every
time it snows, this man clears his own driveway and then he cleans my
father's driveway, and walkway as well. Not only does this kind act touch
my father's heart, but it warms mine as well. I am grateful to know there
are kind people looking out for my father when I can't be there.

*Is there someone you know who needs assistance shoveling their walk, raking
leaves, or cutting their grass?*

_____

_____

_____

_____

_____

"Everybody likes a compliment."

~ Abraham Lincoln

4

**Practice the one-in/one-out rule. Each time you
get a new item of clothing or pair of shoes, donate
something you haven't worn in a while to charity.**

We live in a world of consumerism, materialism, and over-abundance. It seems as though we measure success by how many "things" we acquire, including the latest fashions. I am guilty of owning too many clothes and shoes, some of which I never wear. There are so many people who have only one pair of shoes, one coat and limited clothing. Several years ago, I started practicing what a dear friend termed "the one-in/one-out rule."

Every time I purchase a new pair of shoes, I donate an existing pair to a charitable organization. I practice this with items of clothing as well. It helps me to keep my closet free of clutter and aid someone in need at the same time.

Even if you don't make a new purchase, you can purge your closet at least twice a year. Gently used jeans, footwear, sweaters, warm coats, scarves, hats, and mittens are always in need. If you can't get out of the house to donate, many organizations will come to your home to pick up bagged or boxed items.

What do you have in your home that hasn't been used in over a year? What charitable organization could you call to come pick it up?

_____

_____

_____

_____

_____

5

**Send a letter or card in the mail to a child in your life
(your child, niece, nephew, grandchild or godchild).
They love to get mail and it will brighten their day!**

Do you remember when you were a kid and your job was to go down to the mailbox to collect the mail? I do! I was always so excited and couldn't understand why my parents didn't feel the same way. Little did I realize that it was mostly bills and advertisements! I just remember hoping to find something with my name on it. Come on, admit it - didn't you do the same thing?

With this in mind, I started sending my 10-year-old niece random cards and letters in the mail. She's too young to have an email address or a telephone at this age, so this is a good way for us to keep in touch. The first card she received from me was a huge surprise! My sister said it made her day. She couldn't stop smiling and talked about it right up until her bed time.

I just sent my niece and nephew Halloween cards because I wasn't able to see them go out trick or treating. If you don't already, consider sending the children in your life a card or note for holidays other than their birthday. It will certainly surprise them and put a smile on their face if they receive a card for Groundhog's Day or the Fourth of July!

In my first card, I asked my niece to become pen-pals. I have to say, when I open the mailbox, I feel like a kid again - waiting for something special with my name on it!

Is there a young child or teen in your life? Send them a surprise card or letter in the mail and see what response you get!

_____

_____

_____

_____

_____

6

❧

**When visiting a friend or relative who has been in
the hospital for an extended period of time, drop off
some food at the nurses' station on their floor.**

My siblings and I dropped off baskets of goodies to the oncology
nurses who had cared for my mother during the last two-weeks of her life.
They were extremely touched.

My friend and her sister-in-law made bags of Hershey's "hugs & kisses"
for their mother's nurses while she was sick in the hospital. The candy bags
included a picture of her mother, so the nurses could associate the treat
with the patient. Even though this might be considered a nurse's job, it
is always important to appreciate care givers. This applies to the vet staff
caring for your pet as well!

*Is there a local hospital, doctor's office or vet you visit frequently? What could
you drop off for the staff to say thank-you for all of the care you've received
over the years?*

_____

_____

_____

_____

_____

*"No act of kindness, no matter
how small, is ever wasted."*

~ Aesop

7

If your building has a doorman/receptionist, bring him/her a cup of coffee or tea on occasion.

Every day I used to pass the same front desk receptionist on my way into work. Many people just rushed on by, in a hurry to get to their office. I always stopped to say hello, call her by name, and occasionally bring her a cup of coffee. Think about it…this person is stuck behind the desk (or opening the door) for long hours at a time. They might not have the luxury of grabbing a cup of coffee whenever they want. The simple gift of a beverage will let them know you appreciate them, don't take them for granted, and understand their situation.

Who do you pass on a daily basis that might enjoy a surprise to brighten their day?

_____

_____

_____

_____

_____

"My religion is very simple. My religion is kindness."

~ Dalai Lama

8

**Leave a note in your child's lunch bag telling them
you love them and wish them a wonderful day!**

Several years ago, I was living with a man whose young son who spent half
of his time living with us, and the other half with his mother. When he started
first grade he was full of excitement, yet nervous and a little apprehensive. To
help him feel more at ease, I began writing little notes of encouragement and
leaving them in his lunch bag or book bag to discover throughout his day.

Sometimes I addressed a certain issue, such as "Good luck on your
spelling quiz" or "Have fun in gym class today." Other times I simply told
him "Enjoy your day. I love you. XO" It was my way of giving him a hug
from afar and helping him through feelings of loneliness.

Imagine my surprise one day as I opened my briefcase at work and found
a note written in his child-like handwriting. It read "Have a fun day at work.
I love you! XOXOXOXOX!!!" Our note exchange continued for over a year.

I like to believe I had created a feeling of love and appreciation in him,
which he would be able to carry on throughout his life. Six months after
I moved out of the home we shared, I received a Valentine's Day card and
hand-painted garden flag he had made for me. His card expressed how much
he missed me and loved me - and he had filled the page with X's and O's!

Take the time to leave surprise notes for your children, affirming your
love and letting them know you are thinking of them. You never know
what emotions they might be going through at the time of discovery, but
I can guarantee it will bring a smile to their face!

*Commit to surprising your child, spouse, partner, or roommate with a surprise
note of appreciation. What will you say? Where will you hide it?*

_____

_____

_____

_____

_____

Smile at people you pass on the street or in stores. Not only will you bring happiness to their day, but yours as well.

When passing by someone, smile, look them in the eyes, and say hello. Too many people look straight ahead or cast their eyes downward when passing another, as if they are invisible. We are all on this planet for a limited time. Why not make the most of every situation to brighten someone's day?

You never know what someone is going through or whether they have anyone in their life to talk to. It doesn't take long and the benefits are endless. I have met numerous people this way, formed lasting friendships and when I was single, even ended up with a few dates!

And always smile at babies…they smile back!

How many people can you smile at in one day? Make it a challenge! Write down a number and come back here to enter the actual amount at the end of the day.

_____

_____

_____

_____

_____

*"The best way to find yourself is to lose
yourself in the service of others."*

~ Mahatma Gandhi

Stop and hold the door for the person behind you – regardless of their age or gender.

I always hold the door for the person going in behind me and sometimes those coming out as well! It doesn't really matter whether it's woman or a man. I have noticed that the gentlemen might be a little shy about this act.

One day, a scowling, grumpy-looking senior was behind me. I held the door for him, smiled, and said hello. He looked surprised, but brightened up, immediately took the door from me, and held it for five other people entering the building. I even heard him say a gruff hello to one of the women. I like to think I changed his mood that day.

Think of a time you held the door for someone without even thinking about it. Did you notice a change in their attitude or mood afterward?

"Life is mostly froth & bubble; two things stand in stone: Kindness in another's trouble, Courage in your own."

~ Adam Lindsay Gordon

11

If you have an elderly neighbor, stop by on your way to the grocery store and ask if there is anything they might need.

My neighbor, a single woman in her late 70's who walked with a cane, was rear-ended in a traffic accident. Although she was shaken and sore, she would be okay after undergoing a few weeks of physical therapy for injuries to her neck and back.

Her car, on the other hand, didn't fare as well. It was in the shop for over a week when the insurance company declared it a total loss. Her nephew began the hunt for a used car that would work with her special needs. While she was able to get a community transportation service to take her to physical therapy, she had no way of getting to the grocery store.

Noticing this, I offered to pick up some groceries for her on my weekly shopping trip. Not wanting to be a bother, she only asked me to buy her some bread and milk. I assured her it was not an inconvenience and that I was happy to help. I insisted she needed fresh fruit, vegetables, canned goods, and protein as well. Her items only filled one extra bag and were not difficult for me to collect while I was buying the same things. I will never forget the look of gratitude on her face when I brought them to her door.

Take a moment to observe your neighbors and see if there is a need you can fill. You will be flooded with good feelings and the satisfaction of helping another while providing very real necessities.

Take notice of your neighbors on a daily basis. Is there someone who is in need of some basic necessities? How could you offer your assistance?

_____

_____

_____

_____

_____

If you see someone in the grocery store struggling to reach something from the top shelf, offer to get it for them.

Once when I was shopping for groceries in a frenzied rush, I came down the pasta aisle and saw an elderly woman get off of her motorized scooter. She stepped onto the lowest shelf in order to reach a jar of spaghetti sauce on the top shelf. I could see this might not go well as she teetered unsteadily.

I quickly walked up to her and asked her if I could get the jar for her. She turned to me in surprise, gave me a warm smile and a hearty thank you...a very nice reward for an easy task. I walked away feeling calmer than when I had entered the store.

Keep your eyes open for ways you could help someone else while out running errands today. Come back here and make note of your good deeds.

"To practice five things under all circumstances constitutes perfect virtue; these five are gravity, generosity of soul, sincerity, earnestness, and kindness."

~ Confucius

Ask your waiter/waitress how their day is going, use their name when ordering, and thank them when they bring something to the table. They will feel recognized as a person, not just a servant.

As a former waitress, I remember how it felt when customers treated me as nothing but a servant. Although I was there to serve them, I often dealt with rude, belittling behavior. Many people believe they are paying for the service, so they can act any way they choose. Remember, this is another human being, who is trying to make a living.

Now as a customer, I always listen when the wait staff comes to the table to introduce themselves and I immediately use their name so that I won't forget it. I make sure to call them by name when ordering, asking for something extra, or thanking them. One waitress serving us on a busy Father's Day weekend, said "Thank you for remembering my name. Not many people do and that felt great."

During a long arduous shift, simply recognizing them as a person, making a connection, and interacting with them will make for a much more pleasant day. And trust me, you will get much better service!

Think about the last time you ate out. Did you even listen when the waiter/ waitress told you their name? How might you become better at recognizing them and making them feel appreciated?

_____

_____

_____

_____

_____

"Guard well within yourself that treasure,
kindness. Know how to give without
hesitation, how to lose without regret,
how to acquire without meanness."

~ George Sand

Winter can be rough. Even if your roads and parking lot are cleared by a service, the cars will still be covered in snow and need clearing. Clear your neighbor's car while you are clearing your own.

My condominium complex pays a service to clear the steps, walkways, and parking lot when it snows. However, we still have to clear the snow off our own cars. That might not sound like a difficult task – until you realize we often get 8-12" of snow in one storm!

My four-foot, long-handled, rubber snow brush makes clearing the snow off the roof of the car much faster and less arduous. On many occasions, I have cleared my own car and then cleared the snow from the cars of several single, elderly women.

I keep the brush in a common closet in the condo foyer. After one particularly heavy storm, I witnessed my neighbor, a gruff man who always kept to himself, use my snow brush to clear off his car, then my car, and that of three other neighbors!

It became a regular practice for everyone to share that brush and look after another neighbor or two. It's as though brotherly love and selflessness flowed through that snow brush all winter long. In a time when people rarely know their neighbors, it was nice to feel part of a tight-knit, caring community.

How might you look after your neighbors and create a sense of community in your neighborhood? Who could you enlist to help you? Write down a few names and commit to contacting them.

_____

_____

_____

_____

_____

"*Kindness in ourselves is the honey that
blunts the sting of unkindness in another.*"

~ Walter Savage Landor

Say hello and chat with the grocery store clerk, looking them in the eyes as they ring up your order. It will brighten their day and make it go much faster.

Think about that person standing behind the conveyor belt as they ring up your milk, broccoli, chicken, paper goods, and orange juice, etc. For the majority of the day, their gaze is cast downward at an array of grocery items sliding past them. I bet they could name all of the items they saw that day, but not recognize one face that stood before them. Most customers are busy unloading their cart full of purchases onto the belt and barely look at the other human being just inches from them.

I consciously stand before them, look into their eyes, and ask how their day is going. Sometimes they give me a pat answer, like "fine" or "okay." But many times they will tell me things like "It's going great. I'm done in an hour and then I get to go to a party" or "It's kind of tough because my cat has been sick and I'm worried about her." We then spend a few minutes chatting about their life – or mine – while the groceries get scanned and bagged. Standing there for hours on end can feel tedious and thankless. Spend some time to make the person in front of you feel valued; your mood will be uplifted as well.

The next time you are in a checkout line at the store, what will you say to the clerk? How could you make them feel seen that day?

_____

_____

_____

_____

_____

16

If you have a delivery or repair person coming to your home, be friendly, use their name, and ask how their day is going. If it is a hot day, offer them a drink of water. I can guarantee you will receive much better service.

I have moved over 17 times in 27 years, and I've seen a lot of movers, delivery persons, contractors and repair persons. The first thing I do is ask their name, and then I use it several times when addressing them. This personalizes the experience and allows for better connection. Let's face it, most people like to hear their own name. You will make them feel more valuable and appreciated.

If my move occurs early in the morning, I usually get a box of donut holes for the men to grab a quick bite on their way in or out. Being paid by the hour, they have never taken advantage of it by taking a break. Instead, I find most wait until they are in the truck driving to the final destination to "chow down." Numerous movers have been so appreciative of this gesture that they took extra special care with my belongings and even assisted me with non-moving duties. When the long day is over, I always feel like I have made new friends.

I also routinely have bottles of cold water available to offer the countless workers, contractors, and delivery persons who must come to a new residence. The look of surprise and gratitude that comes across their face, just by offering a cold drink, is immensely rewarding. I like to think that a day of routine stops was brightened by their visit with me.

Do you have service workers come to your home or office? What can you offer them to show that you appreciate their service?

_____

_____

_____

_____

_____

17

Hold the elevator door for someone running to catch it. An extra minute won't make you late and it just might save someone's day!

Have you ever been rushing to get to work or an appointment and it feels as though the elevator is taking hours to arrive? You keep pushing the button over and over, but it doesn't make it come any faster. When it finally arrives and the doors open, you jump in, punch your floor number, and breathe a sigh of relief.

But what happens when you see or hear someone else running to catch it? Do you frantically push the "close door" button or do you hold it for them? Think about it. If it were you a minute ago, wouldn't you want someone to hold the door for you?

As long as it is not filled to capacity, I hold the door for someone rushing to get in an elevator, safe in the knowledge that I helped to make their day brighter. On one occasion, a breathless woman thanked me effusively and told me she was afraid she was going to be late to a first interview. I hope she got the job!

Challenge: How many people can you hold the elevator for in one week?

_____

_____

_____

_____

_____

"Three things in human life are important:
The first is to be kind;
The second is to be kind;
and the third is to be kind."
~ Henry James

When passing a blind person on the street or in a store, say hello.

Every time I pass someone, I smile and say hello, particularly with a blind person. Just because they can't see *you*, doesn't mean they don't know you are in their presence. A simple hello brings a moment of visibility, light, and *recognition* into their life. It's even better if you have the time to chat for a minute or two! The act of making another human feel *seen* is incredibly rewarding and undervalued today.

Have you ever passed a blind person and said nothing? How might it change their day if you said hello? How might it change your own?

_____

_____

_____

_____

_____

*"Kindness and faithfulness keep a king safe,
through kindness his throne is made secure."*

~ King Solomon

19

Buy a hot meal for a homeless person you pass on the street. Even a cup of soup would be welcomed.

If you visit any city, you are likely to see a homeless person sitting on a sidewalk or park bench. Some may be asking for money, while others are simply sleeping, too cautious to fall into slumber at night. Do not judge them; you know nothing about the circumstances that put them there.

Rather than pass this person by as though you don't see them, offer them a meal, a cup of soup, or even hot coffee. Spend a few moments to ask their name and talk to them. Human connection is extremely important to everyone's well-being.

I have purchased sandwiches, soup, and even pizza for homeless persons. When I walk up to them I introduce myself, say hello, and ask their name. Then I say "Hi John, I thought you might like something hot to eat today." The look of gratitude is worth more than the $5-$10 you might spend.

If you pass a homeless person on a regular basis, think about what you could offer them instead of money. Is there a nearby coffee shop or restaurant where you could purchase coffee, soup, or a sandwich?

_____

_____

_____

_____

_____

"Kindness is in our power, even when fondness is not."

~ Samuel Johnson

20

If you routinely go out to lunch, ask your assistant or other office co-worker (who might be stuck behind a desk all day) if you could bring them something when you return. Better yet, just surprise them.

In almost every office where I have worked, there were co-workers who were stuck behind a desk and could not leave during lunch time. If they did get out, their break was spent running errands for their boss or family. These are usually dedicated workers who don't always take time to eat or they grab something unhealthy from the vending machine.

I remember offering to bring food back to one particular assistant who worked through her lunch time every day, so she could leave early to pick up her children. She always politely declined. One day I overheard her telling another co-worker at the coffee machine that she'd forgotten her lunch and would have to "raid the vending machine." Having planned to run out to pick up a salad for myself anyway, I simply picked up two. I offered the salad to her when I returned, saying "I got an extra, would you like it?" The look of surprise, joy, and humble acceptance on her face gave me an instant mood lift that day as well.

Think about your office staff. Is there someone who never gets out at lunch time? What surprise could you bring him/her?

_____

_____

_____

_____

_____

"A tree is known by its fruit; a man by his deeds. A good deed is never lost; he who sows courtesy reaps friendship, and he who plants kindness gathers love."

~ Saint Basil

21

If you are baking during the holidays, make a few extra goodies for someone who isn't expecting to receive treats from you.

I bake cookies and miniature loaves of banana bread for my postal carrier every year, even though I cannot eat them myself due to a gluten allergy. The simple act of giving a homemade treat to a service person is extremely personal. They will appreciate the treat and know you appreciate their service all year long.

Do you have someone in your life who performs a service that you could recognize in a special way during the holidays?

_____

_____

_____

_____

_____

*"Wherever there is a human being, there
is an opportunity for a kindness."*

~ Lucius Annaeus Seneca

22

Make a roast with vegetables and divide it into several containers. Take them to a parent or elderly neighbor to put in their freezer. They will have a nutritious, home-cooked meal ready when they need it.

My father has always been a meat and potatoes lover. Now that my mother has passed away, he misses her cooking. Although I've cooked many things for him, his favorite meal is an old-fashioned roast.

During the fall and winter months, I often cook a roast in the oven with lots of carrots, potatoes, and onions (*lots* of onions!) just for my father. I keep a small portion for myself, but I batch up the rest into three freezer-safe containers for him. I usually put one in his refrigerator for that evening and label the others before placing them in his freezer. He has never been much of a cook himself and relies on frozen dinners, pasta, or eating out at the diner with his buddies. I feel good knowing that he has something nutritious without a lot of preservatives.

I have also done this for some of my elderly neighbors who I know aren't up to cooking like they used to. Their appreciation is monumental for an act that really requires little effort. Give it a try yourself one day soon!

Who in your life would appreciate a home-cooked meal in the next few weeks? Write down their name and what it will be – then commit to it!

_____

_____

_____

_____

_____

23

**Make homemade chicken noodle soup for a sick
friend and drop it off unexpectedly.**

I have a dear friend who is always doing things for others. She has nine children and twenty-three grandchildren, so she is one busy lady! This never stops her from giving to her friends, community, and fellow church members.

One day she came down with a high fever, body aches, and a sore throat. She was unable to leave the house. Her husband travels and was away that week. I was concerned about her being able to care for herself and getting something nutritious to eat. Having just cooked a whole chicken the day before, I decided to make homemade chicken noodle soup for her. What is special about that, you ask? Well, I've never made homemade soup before!

I followed three separate recipes, using the veggies I had on hand: carrots, celery, onion, and corn. Luckily, I also had regular noodles (I'm gluten-free, so I don't usually buy regular pasta). After boiling the chicken carcass in water, I removed it and added some chicken stock, along with vegetables and seasonings. I let it simmer for a while and tasted it. It came out well, but I felt like it was missing something. Not knowing what else to add to it, I let it cool down before placing it in a container and dropping it at her house with some crackers.

The next night, my friend called to tell me how much she appreciated the soup. She had some for dinner that night and again for lunch the following day. She said it was the best soup she had ever tasted! I told her it was my first attempt at homemade chicken noodle soup and she replied "It was so good because it was made with LOVE."

Do you have a sick friend who could use a little extra loving care right now? What can you take them to cheer them up?

_____

_____

_____

_____

_____

24

**If you know a new mom, offer to watch the baby
while she runs an errand – or just showers or naps –
giving her some much needed personal time.**

Mothers of newborns are extremely busy with the baby's constant demands. Trying to take care of a baby, their home, themselves, do laundry, and make meals when they are sleep deprived is incredibly hard.

I know several friends who have said they often didn't get a chance in the day to shower, comb their hair (let alone wash it), or eat. First time mothers – or any new mom – can really use help getting used to the schedule and keeping up with the additional workload.

I had a friend who was a stay-at-home mother and whose children were all in school. When several of her friends started having babies, she knew what they were dealing with. She would often go over to watch the baby, so the fatigued new mom could take a shower or a nap. It may seem like a small act, but it will mean so much to a woman who is in need of some personal time….or sleep!

Do you know a friend or relative who just had a baby and might like a brief reprieve? Send them an email or text to see how you could help out.

_____

_____

_____

_____

"You don't need a reason to help people."
~ Charles Dickens

25

Bring fruit, donuts, or bagels to the office staff on occasion.

I once had a co-worker who always stopped on his way in on Friday mornings to bring something for the entire staff as a "TGIF" celebration. Sometimes he brought donuts, other times it was bagels or fruit. One time he surprised us with hot, soft pretzels!

It really didn't matter what he brought, we would have appreciated it. The fact that he thought of us and wanted to make our Fridays feel special was reward enough.

When this particular employee got promoted, we had a surprise going away party for him, which I know touched his heart. We would miss this giving soul. The very next Friday after his departure, three of the remaining five staff brought in goodies for the group. They all wanted to carry on his act of giving!

What treat could you bring to the office that would improve employee morale? Write down the item and the day you commit to do it.

_____

_____

_____

_____

_____

*"A part of kindness consists in loving
people more than they deserve."*

~ Joseph Joubert

26

If you sit at a restaurant table for two hours or more, tip the wait staff more than 20%, as they would normally have had another customer or two in that time frame.

Having worked through high school and college as a waitress, I know how frustrating it can be when that one table sits for hours, even after their meal is finished and the bill is paid. When you do that, you are taking the space of at least one, if not two more paying customers. It's called "turning over the table" in restaurant lingo. New customers bring in more income for the restaurant and for the wait staff (in the form of a tip).

I love to go out with my friends monthly and catch up on everything going on in their lives. These dinners can sometimes run for three to four hours, as we ladies have a way of talking non-stop. The waiter/waitress could have filled our table and made additional money, if we had not stayed so long. Therefore, I always make sure to leave extra money in the tip. Many of these folks rely on their tips, as the restaurant pays them a very *low* hourly rate (an average of $5 in United States).

When was the last time you gave the wait staff a generous tip? Resolve to give something extra, especially if lingering at the table.

_____

_____

_____

_____

_____

27

Help a friend pack (or unpack) during a move.

It might not seem like a big deal because you've only moved a few times in your life, but I've moved 17 times in 27 years. All of that packing and unpacking gets exhausting. Sure, there's the physical labor of taking things off the walls, emptying drawers, packing the dishes so they won't break, loading books in sturdy boxes, and cleaning out the closets. But there's also an emotional element to moving...especially if you've had to do it a number of times.

Each time you move, it can become a stroll down memory lane as you sort through items in drawers and closets. You get the opportunity to thin out what you no longer need and keep only the things that are important to you.

After many moves, it becomes clear what is really important to take with you the next time and what you can finally release from your life. It helps to have someone with you who can give an unbiased opinion in this regard, and sometimes to give you a hug when you come across pictures of a deceased parent, an old love letter, or memories of a lost relationship.

Helping a friend move is more than just lifting heavy furniture. It's assisting them with a transition in their life.

What can you do to help a friend, co-worker, or relative during their next move? Jot down some ideas and offer them the next time someone mentions they are moving!

_____

_____

_____

_____

"That best portion of a man's life,
his little, nameless, unremembered
acts of kindness and love."

~ William Wordsworth

Drop in unannounced to visit an elderly relative or neighbor who is alone. Bring them a hot cup of coffee or tea and spend a few moments chatting. Or stay longer to play cards or assist them with a chore.

It's easy to get caught up in our own busy, non-stop schedules. Before you know it, the day is over and you didn't finish half of what was on your never-ending to-do list.

However, for some elderly people, the day can stretch on endlessly. Many are active with hobbies, social engagements, friends, and family. Others, due to depression, disability, or lack of transportation, spend the day alone and read or watch television for company.

I have many elderly neighbors in the latter situation. I like to knock on their door on occasion to say hello, bring them some tea, a treat, or just have a chat. On average, it doesn't take a lot of my time (maybe 30 minutes), but it has huge rewards for both of us.

They get socialization and the pleasure of knowing someone cares about them (we all need that). I get the reward of happiness and the knowledge that I helped another human being. Human connection is critical to our well-being. Something as simple as checking in to say hello, and talking (or just listening) to them for a few minutes, can have a huge impact on someone's mood. If you have extra time, you could always stay and play cards or do a task for them.

Who do you know that lives alone and might like a short, friendly visit? Put the person's name & visit date in your telephone calendar. Set an alarm so you won't forget!

_____

_____

_____

_____

"The smallest act of kindness is worth
more than the grandest intention."

~ Oscar Wilde

29

If you see someone trying to merge into traffic in your lane, let them go in front of you. One extra car will not slow you down from reaching your destination.

I think there is too much road rage in the world today. Much of it stems from the over-stressed, fast-paced lifestyle we lead. It doesn't have to be that way.

When a car is trying to merge into traffic from an on-ramp or even from a parking lot along the road, I always let them go in front of me. I know that if I were the driver of that car, I would hope that someone would be kind enough to let me merge into traffic. Sometimes this seems to annoy the car behind me and they honk their car horn at me for sitting still while I let the other car out.

I do not understand why some drivers have to keep edging forward so as not to leave a gap between the car in front of them and their own car. I wonder what they think they are achieving. Or they stare straight ahead and pretend they don't see the other driver.

One extra car will not delay your trip home, to work, to a date, or even to catch a flight! Please be kind to each other on the road!

Will it really ruin your day to let the next person trying to merge go in front of you? Can you commit to trying it for one week?

_____

_____

_____

_____

_____

"A little thought & a little kindness are often worth more than a great deal of money."

~ John Ruskin

30

Keep an extra umbrella in your car or office. Loan
it out on rainy days to those who forgot one.

My mother always told me to keep an extra umbrella in the car in case
I were to forget mine or leave mine behind somewhere. I also kept one in
my office in case it began to rain after I was already in the building.

I found this to be a benefit for my coworkers who needed to head out
during the day on an errand or for lunch. Whenever I heard someone say
"Oh darn, it's raining and I don't have an umbrella with me," I would
happily offer mine. I never labeled it; I trusted people to return it – and
they always did.

People are usually shocked that I offer help before I'm asked. If I hear
someone express a need, I try to fill it if it's within my means. In this case,
an extra umbrella is simple!

*Is there something you could keep on hand at the office or school to loan to
another in need? Would you still do it if you might not get it back?*

_____

_____

_____

_____

_____

"Deliberately seek opportunities for kindness, sympathy, and patience."

~ Evelyn Underhill

31

Randomly text a kind note to a friend or family member.

Sending a letter in the mail used to be a great way to stay in touch with family and friends. Then came email and many people abandoned letter writing. Texting is the new instant form of communication.

Our days can get pretty hectic and stressed. Wouldn't it be a welcome break to read something positive and uplifting during the day? A thoughtful note of appreciation goes a long way to brightening the day for both the sender and the receiver. Send an unexpected text to someone special in your life to say hello, let them know you were thinking of them, and tell them something you appreciate about them.

How does it feel when you receive an unexpected text "just because" the person was thinking of you? Pretty good, right? Commit to sending at least one thoughtful text a week. Jot some names down here!

_____

_____

_____

_____

_____

"Kindness is a language that the deaf
can hear and the blind can see."

~ Mark Twain

32

If you know someone who will be having surgery, take a meal over to them when they return from the hospital. You can schedule a certain night or drop off a frozen home-cooked meal they can just defrost, heat, and enjoy!

Surgery can be scary. Not just because of the risks and complications that might be involved, but also because it makes you feel vulnerable and unsure of the future. If you have never had surgery, be thankful.

Please know that for those of us who have, just having a friend call and check in is a huge comfort. Having someone think ahead and make a meal for you is even better. After surgery, people are weak, in pain, emotionally a little shaky, and have no desire or energy to cook.

I had a friend do this for me when I had two major kidney operations. Barely able to stand afterward, there was no way I could have gotten the nourishment I needed, and that lasagna tasted 100 times better because it was a gift of love.

After this kind gesture was done for me, I began doing the same for many of my friends and family. It is particularly helpful to someone who is single and living alone.

Is there someone you know who is scheduled for surgery? Even if it's an outpatient procedure, they might be groggy from the anesthesia and would appreciate a meal that day!

_____

_____

_____

_____

"The great acts of love are done by those who are habitually doing small acts of kindness."

~ Victor Hugo

33

**If you have great service at a restaurant, store
or other business, tell the manager.**

You've probably heard that positive reinforcement goes a long way and you're probably well acquainted with negative feedback at work or home. Negative feedback is often swift in coming, and the positive feedback may come rarely or almost never.

You can change that within your circle of influence.

The next time you receive great service by a customer service representative of any kind, first tell the person…and then tell their manager. You have no idea the impact it will have on the employee's self-esteem. This good feeling will carry forward to the next customer they serve.

Have you given a service provider praise lately? Commit to taking a few extra minutes to tell their boss the next time!

_____

_____

_____

_____

_____

"Tenderness and kindness are not signs of
weakness or despair, but manifestations
of strength and resolution."

~ Kahlil Gibran

34

Greet people by name whenever you can, especially those you see every day, like a doorman, front receptionist, or security guard.

There's nothing better than hearing your own name. It's nice to be acknowledged in general terms, but when it's personalized with your name, it's even better.

Now think of the front desk clerk in your building sitting there all day with perhaps hundreds of people passing by. Most people rarely look up to say hello as they pass, as if the human being sitting there is part of the furniture! Because the clerk is stationed there, they don't get the normal social interaction that other employees do.

Camaraderie in a work place is not only a nice perk; the human connection is healthy for our well-being. So next time you pass by someone stationed at a front post, please take a few minutes to pause, say hello, include their first name, and ask how their day is going. Then listen. It's that easy and only takes few extra minutes.

Whose name have you been neglecting to use when greeting? If you have trouble with names, keep a note in your telephone, and the next time you say hello, use it!

_____

_____

_____

_____

"*Kindness in words creates confidence.*
Kindness in thinking creates profoundness.
Kindness in giving creates love."
~ Lao Tzu

35

If you have a friend or co-worker who will be alone during the holidays, invite them to dine with your family.

Having moved regularly for most of my adult life, I have often been alone in a new city during a major holiday. Each time I was fortunate enough to make friends who treated me like family.

One of my nicest memories was when my boss invited me to her family's Thanksgiving dinner. She even included a small gift of a beautifully wrapped scented soap beside my plate.

The following Christmas Eve, I lost power and was waiting for the electric company to come and figure out the problem. They ended up digging up my front yard most of the night in order to get to the underground electrical supply. I was stuck in my cold, dark house and couldn't leave to attend a friend's party.

My neighbors were gracious enough to ask me to join their extended family for dinner, caroling and presents. When my power was still out at bedtime, they invited me to stay the night. Having a full house of guests, I marveled at the generosity of their offer. My eyes filled with tears at this act of kindness.

Which single friend, co-worker or relative might you invite to your next holiday gathering?

_____

_____

_____

_____

_____

36

If you have extra coupons for store sales or items you won't be buying, offer them to a fellow shopper.

I have always been a huge fan of coupons, something passed down to me by my late mother. While grocery shopping, if I have the paper coupons with me and decide not to buy something, I place the coupon on the shelf next to the item. It makes me happy to think that someone else will be able to save the money on their purchase.

Stores often send out coupons for secret sales to customers who have signed up for their rewards card. If you're in the store, but decide not to make a purchase that day, offer the coupon to someone who didn't receive it, so that they can save the money. Their look of surprise, elation and gratitude is always worth it!

This kind act of giving to others has been returned to me several times. I've had people offer me coupons for 20% off my entire purchase, free coffee, and even a ticket for free admission to a rodeo. We get back what we put out in life.

Do you have any unused discounts, passes, or freebies you could you offer someone else this month?

_____

_____

_____

_____

_____

*"Kindness makes a fellow feel good whether
it's being done to him or by him."*

~ Frank A. Clark

37

Offer to take the picture of a group or couple who appear to be tourists – or who you see trying to take a "selfie." The picture will come out nicer and they will usually offer to take yours in return.

How many times have you been somewhere with a friend or family member trying to capture that "Kodak moment" of yourselves in front of a beautiful landscape, historic monument, or other important setting? Didn't you wish you had someone to take the picture for you?

Think about that the next time you see someone else in the same situation. Take a few minutes and offer to capture that moment for them - even if you don't need them to return the favor. It's one of the nicest things you can do for a stranger and perhaps you will make a new friend from a different country in the process.

Do you travel regularly? If not, perhaps you live in a city that receives frequent tourists. Make it a point to offer to take a fellow traveler's picture next time

_____

_____

_____

_____

_____

"A generous heart, kind speech, and
a life of service and compassion are
the things that renew humanity."

~ Guatama Buddha

38

**If someone looks lost or confused, don't wait for
them to ask for help - offer directions.**

I once worked in an office park that was laid out in a very confusing manner. While the setting was gorgeous, it was difficult to find the building you wanted if you didn't know where you were going. Not only were there four entrances to the complex, but there were many curving roads that looped around buildings which were set at every angle. It was almost like driving through a maze. The building numbers were also placed very high by the roof line and only on one side of the building. To make things more difficult, the map for the complex was at the front entrance, so once you were inside the complex, there were no other signs to help you find your way.

While out walking on my lunch hour, I would often see cars creeping along slowly, the drivers craning their necks to look up at the number on the top of the building. I knew they were lost. I would usually wave to the person and ask, "Do you need help?" Invariably, they would. After giving them the easiest method of getting to their destination, their look of relief and gratitude was reward enough.

I could have kept walking, saying to myself "This is my lunch hour; I only get a limited time to myself." But in truth, it only took an average of one minute to help another human being. And chances are, I prevented them from being late for an interview or appointment. That always made me feel it was worth my time.

In what ways could you be more present for the people around you and offer assistance where needed?

_____

_____

_____

_____

_____

39

Stop at a child's lemonade stand and buy a drink.

When you were a kid, did you have dreams of making your own money? Did you get your mother to help you mix the lemonade and set up the table, writing the sign in your childish print? Remember the excitement and anticipation of having a customer stop and purchase a small glass of lemonade from you? It was invigorating to think that you could actually do something to generate income when you were under the age of 10!

Although the price has risen from $.25 to $1.00 these days, I always stop and buy from the enterprising young children I pass. This isn't just about kids making money, it's a lesson in self-promotion and entrepreneurialism. Your purchase is a way of acknowledging their efforts to be self-sufficient.

The little girls who live next door recently put up a stand to sell pink lemonade for $1.00. Although it was warm and sickly sweet, their proud smiles of delight when I stopped to buy one brightened my day.

Do you have enterprising children in your community? In what ways could you support their efforts?

_____

_____

_____

_____

_____

40

Don't just ask someone 'How are you?' without meaning it. Really listen to someone's troubles or need to share that day.

We often ask this question as a form of greeting without really caring what the other person replies - or worse, we expect them to just say "fine," and we keep moving.

One day after greeting a co-worker with this phrase on the way into my building several years ago, I got an honest answer. She replied, "I'm not doing so great. My ex-husband hasn't paid my child support in months, my washing machine broke last night, and now I think I'm getting the flu."

That made me stop in my tracks.

I realized she needed to vent to someone. I stopped and told her I was sorry to hear these things. It opened up the flood gates and she unloaded her troubles on me for five minutes. I just stood there giving her my full attention, listening and nodding.

After she finished, she said, "Thank you for taking the time to listen to me. I didn't mean to go off like that, but it's been building up inside. I feel better just getting it out." She smiled and gave me a hug. The whole exchange only took a few minutes, but it made a huge impact on my co-worker's day. The memory has stuck with me all this time and I realized the power of just listening.

Is there someone you could spend a few minutes chatting with in order to make them feel seen or heard that day?

_____

_____

_____

_____

_____

"Those who bring sunshine to the lives of others cannot keep it from themselves."

~ Sir James M. Barrie

41

If you live in a town with coin parking meters, put some coins in a meter that's about to expire. You'll make someone's day for under a dollar!

Have you ever been held up in an appointment and panicked knowing the parking meter was going to expire? Like me, you probably prayed you'd get to your car before parking enforcement got there to ticket your car.

I remember running into a store to make a quick return only to find a long line. I agonized over the decision to return to my car to put more money in the meter or stay in line and chance the ticket. I stayed in line... and ended up being 20 minutes over the time limit.

When I ran out to the car, I was surprised to see another full hour on the meter! Someone had come by and put extra money in the meter for me. I felt a mix of relief, surprise and delight. From that day on I vowed to always carry extra change and pass the favor on to another person.

Where could you offer someone minor monetary assistance? Could you put money in a parking meter? Pay a toll? Cover a load of wash at the laundromat?

_____

_____

_____

_____

_____

42

Pick up trash on the street or in your complex rather than walking past it. This will make the world a more beautiful place.

Almost every day as I walk my dog, I find trash or recycling products that have blown over from the collection receptacles in my condominium complex. I stop to pick up the various items caught in the bushes or lying on the sidewalks.

It doesn't matter that the trash is in front of buildings other than my own. I feel a sense of responsibility to make the *entire* development a lovelier place. As long as I am walking by, why not be kind to the environment, and my neighbors, by picking up the trash? This is something easy that you can do to make your personal environment and the planet a better, more beautiful place.

Do you notice trash in your complex at home, work, or school? Could you make a point to pick it up whenever you see it? You just might set the example for others observing your good deed.

_____

_____

_____

_____

_____

"Real kindness seeks no return; what return can the world make to rain clouds?"

~ Thiruvalluvar

43

Leave your newspaper or magazine on the bus/train/plane for the next person to read with a note "enjoy it and pass it on."

I remember boarding a plane for a five-hour direct flight from the East Coast to California. I'd forgotten to pack a book or magazine, and I didn't have a smartphone or iPad at the time. I groaned at the thought that I'd be stuck reading the in-flight magazine repeatedly in order to pass the time. Even with a movie on the flight, I knew I'd be bored to tears.

When I got to my seat, to my surprise and delight, someone had left a magazine in the seat pocket in front of me. There was a note on the front that read, "To help kill time…enjoy." A huge smile spread across my face and I vowed to not only pass on this particular magazine, but carry on the tradition wherever I could. Since that time, I have left plenty of reading materials for others in hopes that the chain would be continued.

Be aware of times when you may have reading material you could leave for the next person on public transportation, in a waiting room, or a cafeteria.

_____

_____

_____

_____

_____

*"What wisdom can you find that
is greater than kindness?"*

~ Jean-Jacques Rousseau

44

**Put your telephone away and give your children/
partner/companion your full attention.**

Today with all the electronic distractions we have, it is often difficult to be present 100% of the time. I know how I have felt when trying to talk with someone who is not making eye contact or is always looking down at their device. I feel as though they are not engaging with me and not really listening to what I am saying.

Quality time, one of the Five Love Languages according to Dr. Gary Chapman, is critical for some individuals to feel loved. The next time you are talking with someone, give them your full, undivided attention. Human connection is vital for us all.

Think about all of the times you've multi-tasked when someone was trying to talk with you. Could you commit to putting your device away for at least one hour and giving your companion your full attention?

_____

_____

_____

_____

_____

"The words of kindness are more healing to a drooping heart than balm or honey."

~ Sarah Fielding

Make eye contact with people you talk to.

This one is perhaps the simplest act of kindness you can do for a person. It is the gift of recognition and acknowledgement. It is a gesture of making the person feel seen, and it conveys a message that they are important.

I make eye contact with people I meet while walking my dog, buying groceries, ordering a meal, picking up my dry cleaning, and when speaking with friends and family. I know it makes me feel valued when someone looks into my eyes, and I'm sure it will have the same effect on others.

Do you regularly make eye contact with the people you engage with — even in the smallest of exchanges? Commit to looking into their eyes the next few times and see how your own mood changes as a result of the contact.

_____

_____

_____

_____

"Compassion is the basis of morality."

~ Arthur Schopenhauer

46

If you see a neighbor walking in the direction of home, stop and offer a ride – especially if they are carrying packages.

I often see my neighbors walking to and from local stores. I know that a few of them have cars and are likely just choosing to get some exercise during the day. However, I have passed several who are carrying bags of groceries and clearly heading home. What started out as exercise may have turned into a burdensome chore.

Even though we all go into a store for a few things, we often come away with much more than we intended. For this reason, I always stop to see if they would prefer a ride the rest of the way. I figure the heavy bags are not making their walk enjoyable at this point and they might like some relief. I'm almost never turned down. I like to think someone would do the same for me one day!

Are you mindful and aware of others in your neighborhood? How could you be more helpful or engaging?

_____

_____

_____

_____

_____

"You cannot do a kindness too soon, for you
never know how soon it will be too late."

~ Ralph Waldo Emerson

47

If you see a homeless person with a dog, give them some dog food in a pop-top can, along with a meal for the owner.

It's important to remember that homeless people aren't always on the streets by choice. They usually have an unforeseen event in their lives that put them there and it's a last resort.

Often these people have pets with them. While some might think it is cruel or a "gimmick" to get sympathy, it's more likely that the person chose not to abandon the pet when their own circumstances took a turn. So many pets are euthanized daily due to overcrowding or being placed in a shelter without a no-kill policy. The person might also feel they need the companionship or protection while living on the streets.

In any case, consider buying one or two cans of dog or cat food with an easy to open pop-top lid. Drop it off, along with a meal for the owner, the next time you pass by.

Have you noticed someone in your town who has fallen on hard times and is trying to care for their pet? Commit to dropping off food or blankets for the animal and his owner.

_____

_____

_____

_____

_____

48

**When you are at the gym, if you notice regulars who
have gotten fit, lost weight, or improved their health,
congratulate them on their achievements.**

Like many people, I've attended a gym regularly for the last several
years. I'm not always capable of doing more than a gentle yoga class,
riding a stationary bike, or lifting light weights. However, there are some
dedicated individuals I see on a regular basis who are clearly working out
hard by running on a treadmill, lifting heavy weights, or sweating off
calories in a Zumba class.

If you are observant, over time you will notice the bodies of regular
members changing for the better. Perhaps they have lost weight, gained
muscle, or they just look plain healthier. Even though I don't know them
all by name, I always take the time to say, "You look great!" or "Your hard
work has paid off!"

I'm positive you'll be rewarded with a great big smile. Wouldn't you
love it if someone recognized the efforts you made?

*Is there someone you see regularly who you know is consciously working on
becoming healthier, exercising and improving their well-being? Let them know
you noticed and congratulate them on the changes they've made, no matter
how small.*

_____

_____

_____

_____

_____

"Shall we make a new rule of life
from tonight: Always to try to be a
little kinder than is necessary."

~ Sir James M. Barrie

49

Talk to someone you see standing alone at a party or gathering. Welcome them into your circle and introduce them around.

Have you ever been invited to a party where you only knew the host or one other guest? I used to be quite shy and awkward at social gatherings where I knew no one. I'd stand by the food or drinks, looking busy and hoping someone would talk to me when they came by.

Now that I am more outgoing, I easily strike up conversations with strangers, but I remember how painful it was for me to stand there alone. With that in mind, I am mindful of others in this predicament whenever I'm at a party, meeting or networking event.

I approach people with a smile and introduce myself. After a few minutes of conversation, the other person often visibly relaxes and I ask them to come join my friends or colleagues. Even if they decline, I know I played a hand in making another human being feel good that day.

At your last social gathering, do you remember seeing someone who appeared to be alone with no one to talk to? What did you do? What could you do the next time you see someone in that situation?

_____

_____

_____

_____

_____

"We must give more in order to get more.
It is the generous giving of ourselves
that produces the generous harvest."

~ Orison Swett Marden

50

**Put positive affirmations inside of library books
for the next person to find unexpectedly.**

Ever since I was a young girl, I have loved to read. I would check out several books from the library at a time. I particularly loved series books written by the same author. I always found myself eagerly anticipating the next book and the feeling of having something to look forward to.

On one particular visit to the library, I remember opening a book and finding a small note from a previous reader that said, "You are a fantastic reader. Keep up the good work."

I was surprised and wondered who had placed it there. Had the inspirational message been in the book for a while and benefited many readers that came before me? Or had the last person who read it decided to brighten the next person's day?

I wasn't sure, but I knew that I would begin the tradition myself. Sometimes I just wrote, "Have a wonderful day!" with a smiley face on it. Other times I would write things like, "You are perfect the way you are." or "You can do whatever you set your mind to."

I know my words must have made someone smile just as wide as I did when I found my first note!

If you don't visit a library, where else might you leave an uplifting note for a stranger to find?

_____

_____

_____

_____

_____

"Kindness should be like breathing....
a natural act of living."

~ Tae Lynne

Afterword

By now you should have noticed a theme running through this book. In my opinion, kindness is about being mindful, present and making a connection with others.

Kindness is not difficult. It is human nature. It's as simple as making another feel seen, heard, understood or cared for.

Open your eyes, your heart, and your mind to all the ways you can touch another person's life. Once you do, it will create a ripple effect and those loving acts of kindness will continue to be spread outward, encircling many others along the way.

Imagine if each person in the world were to take a mere *60 seconds* to be kinder to another living, breathing being and to the environment as well. The ripples could become tidal waves, washing over the planet in love, light, and compassion.

So take your kindness plan and go out and add a splash of color to the world with your love, patience, and generosity. It will surely brighten someone's day, in addition to your own!

You can get my free guide "10 Simple Ways to Make a Difference" on my website www.60SecondsToKindness.com. Learn more ways to help others, even if you have your own physical limitations.

About the Author

Affectionately known as the Kindness Junkie, Tae Lynne is the founder of 60 Seconds to Kindness, and the author of the eBook *Green Smoothies to the Rescue: How Green Smoothies Helped Ease my Gastroparesis, Restored My Strength and Helped Me Thrive*. Her mission is to inspire others to live a more meaningful live through kindness and acceptance.

Tae has triumphed over chronic illness, learning to thrive despite ME/CFS, Fibromyalgia and Gastroparesis. She shares her story of climbing out of severe illness and depression, and her wisdom about the role helping *others* plays in benefitting our *own* well-being.

Tae is also a collaborative author in the best-selling books, *365 Ways to Connect with Your Soul* and *365 Moments of Grace*. Both books contain uplifting, true-life stories from over 200 authors.

Connect with Tae on Twitter or Instagram: @Kindness_Junkie.

Printed in the United States
By Bookmasters